The Lost Coin

A parable of Jesus

Luke 15:8–10, for children

Written by Nicole E. Dreyer

Illustrated by Roberta Collier-Morales

CONCORDIA PUBLISHING HOUSE · SAINT LOUIS

Jesus traveled from town to town
And everywhere He walked,
Crowds would gather and follow Him
To listen as He talked.

The crowds were full of people who
Loved Jesus very much.
They ate with Him and talked with Him
And were blessed by His Words or touch.

But not everyone who followed the Lord
Was happy with what they heard.
They muttered and complained behind His back.
And Jesus heard every word.

The teachers and the Pharisees
Thought Jesus had made a mistake
Because He ate with those who sinned
And collectors with taxes to take.

But Jesus knew these Pharisees
Did not know why He came,
So Jesus told this parable
His gospel to explain:

"Suppose there was a woman who,"
Our Savior began to say,
"Had saved ten silver drachmas—coins—
Each one worth one day's pay.

"But then one day to her surprise
The woman had quite a shock.
One of her coins had disappeared—
Now where could it have dropped?

"The woman's house was very dark—
No windows in any wall.
The floor was earthen—made of dirt—
So the color was rather dull.

"How could she find just one small coin
On a floor made out of dirt?
She lit her lamp, then took her broom,
And swept to begin her search.

"She swept the broom across the floor
And listened for any sound.
Then suddenly she heard the clink
Of her coin there on the ground!

"Oh, what joy the woman felt
To have her coin again!
'I'll celebrate,' the woman thought,
'And invite my neighbors and friends!'

" 'Rejoice with me,' the woman said
To everyone she knew.
'The coin I lost has now been found;
I'll share my joy with you!' "

Now you might think it's rather strange
To party for a coin.
But for this woman it was worth
A treasure chest of joy!

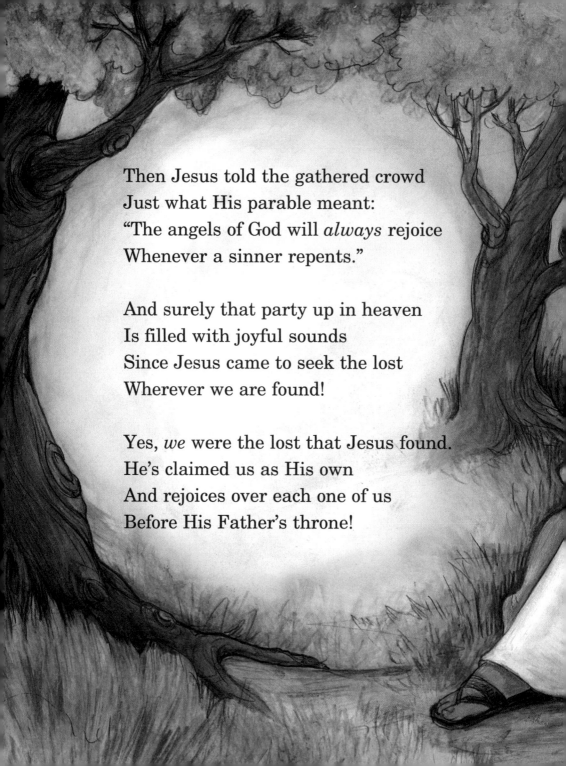

Then Jesus told the gathered crowd
Just what His parable meant:
"The angels of God will *always* rejoice
Whenever a sinner repents."

And surely that party up in heaven
Is filled with joyful sounds
Since Jesus came to seek the lost
Wherever we are found!

Yes, *we* were the lost that Jesus found.
He's claimed us as His own
And rejoices over each one of us
Before His Father's throne!

Dear Parents,

Although we may not be aware of it, many of us can be quick to point out other people's faults. When we do this, we are just like the Pharisees in this story who were critical of Jesus because He associated with sinners. The Parable of the Lost Coin is a reminder to us that Jesus was sent not to condemn those who do wrong, but to save them. This parable tells us that Jesus came to save all of us, not just the people who think they are good because they do good things on earth; therefore: "... there is joy before the angels of God over one sinner who repents" (Luke 15:10).

A person who repents is one who hears God's Law and recognizes his or her own sin. The person is sorry for what he did wrong and resolves to follow God's Word. Redemption comes by God bestowing His forgiveness upon the penitent sinner. This message of redemption is repeated throughout Scripture. Again: "Just so, I tell you, there will be more joy in heaven over one sinner who repents than over ninety-nine righteous persons who need no repentance" (Luke 15:7 ESV).

When you read this story with your child, compare how the woman felt when she found her lost coin to the happiness we feel in recovering something that we missed. Tell your child that every time we do this, we can remember how happy the Lord is when we are "found" by Him and He gives us His forgiveness.

Tell your child that, just as you forgive her when she does wrong things, Jesus forgives us when we ask Him. Explain that because of Jesus' death and resurrection we all, despite our sins, can be saved.

The Editor